# Welcome! A Letter from the Author

Dear Gardening Enthusiasts and Families,

Welcome to Sankofa Sprouts: The Salad Bowl Project! This book is a **step-by-step guide** to the wonderful world of gardening. The book is designed for educational purposes.

Gardening is a wonderful way to nurture well-being, while also teaching patience, responsibility, and the joy of caring for living things. In this book, I provide simple, hands-on activities to help children grow their very own salad bowl garden. I use my experiences as an educator and Master Gardener, along with my expertise in Child and Adolescent Development.

This book is designed to help African American children connect with their rich cultural heritage in gardening and community building. For generations, our ancestors turned to the soil not just to survive, but to cultivate strength, pride, and a deep bond with the earth. My career has focused on supporting the growth and development of African American children and youth. This book reflects both my personal passion and professional commitment.

# Preface

Sankofa Sprouts: The Salad Bowl Project was created to support future generations of growers, thinkers, and builders of community. Sankofa means to carry past lessons into the present and future. This book affirms and reclaims the timeless connection that people of African descent have had to gardening and nature.

Rooted in practical knowledge, this book makes gardening approachable for children. It teaches them how to grow plants with care while also connecting to their cultural roots. Throughout the book there are joyful images of Black children engaging in gardening activities, and relevant Black history tidbits. Children are encouraged to see themselves as part of a legacy of contributors, to not just gardening, but to the environment.

The book promotes gardening success through detailed and accessible guidance. Whether children are new to the garden, or deepening their understanding, the activities promote a range of knowledge and skills that apply to gardening and beyond.

# Introduction

The focus is on growing cherry tomatoes, leaf lettuce, and radish. The book is designed for children in the third and fourth grades. But it could also be helpful for children in the second grade when they are working with older youth or an adult. Fifth graders who want to grow their mentoring skills or enjoy helping younger children can join in too.

Gardening is more than just digging in the dirt. It promotes a host of skills that are beneficial in the short and long term. Gardening has been found to promote children's interest in and practices related to healthful eating. This includes fruits and vegetables. Gardening has also been found to contribute to school achievement, especially in science.

In this book, children are taught how to prepare for planting, and track weather data in a hands-on way. They enter information into tables and think about what the numbers mean for their gardening. Children also learn about soil and climate conditions to make decisions about where and how to plant. They are provided with detailed guidance, prompts, and engaging visuals throughout the book.

# Introduction

Gardening teaches children responsibility. In this book, children are guided to plan and prepare, follow directions, plant and monitor the growth of plants. They are also given information to make decisions about when and how much to water, and when to harvest plants.

Gardening allows children to see the results of their efforts. It promotes a sense of accomplishment. Gardening can also improve mood. Engaging with nature and interacting with the soil can be calming.

The guidance provided is user-friendly. It includes larger, 18-point font and eye-catching visuals. There are chapters on knowing and growing (1) tomatoes, (2) lettuce, and (3) radish. Each of these chapters is further divided into specific sections on how to care for each plant. Examples include making sure plants have enough room to grow, planting, and watering instructions.

Though children will need some support from adults, the aim is to give them enough information to carry out most activities primarily on their own.

# Table of Contents

# What does Sankofa mean?

Sankofa is an Adinkra symbol. It is one of many symbols from West Africa. Adinkra symbols are used to remind us of what Africans believe about how we should live.

The Sankofa symbol says to bring important lessons from the past into the present, and future. It shows a bird looking backwards and picking up a seed. The seed represents knowledge and good-sense lessons we have learned.

Think about a time when you learned something new. What do you remember about what went well? How did this help you do better?

# The Salad Bowl Project

Africans also believe in learning from elders, and from people from the past. This book is about gardening. There are many lessons we can learn from others about gardening. These lessons teach us about how to garden the right way. The lessons also teach us how gardening helps people and the planet.

George Washington Carver was a famous scientist and teacher. He taught us about growing plants in ways that improved the soil. He wanted to make things better for Black farmers and help them do the best they could.

# The Salad Bowl Project

In this book, you will learn about growing three types of foods. These are cherry tomatoes, leaf lettuce, and radish. You will also learn about good practices for gardening.

## Why should you garden?

Gardening is fun! You get to dig in the dirt, take care of the plants, and watch them grow. Gardening also helps to improve the soil. When the soil is healthy, it holds more water. Gardening then helps to save water.

Plants also improve the air. Plants take in pollution and produce oxygen. Gardening helps feed people. You, your friends, and family can eat the food you grow.

# Booker T. Whatley

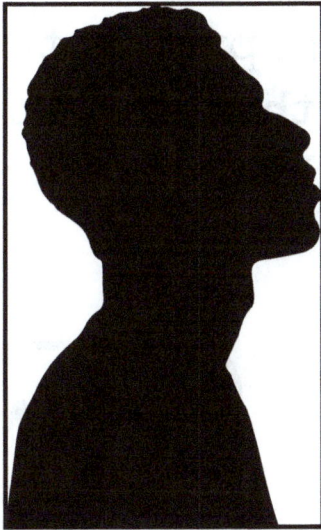

Booker T. Whatley taught Black farmers about planning and good sense farming. He helped farmers see they could make more money by working with and selling to people in the community. That way, Black farmers would not have to just depend on grocery stores to sell their goods. Booker T. Whatley also taught farming in ways that helped the soil. With healthy soil, farmers could get more **yield**.

**Yield** is what you get back based on what you do. One example of a high yield is planting ten seeds and getting ten big plants in return.

# Plan| Prepare| Take Action

A high yield requires a good plan, preparation, and good-sense actions. **Planning** is **thinking ahead** about what you will need, and what actions you need to take.

With gardening you need plants or seeds, soil, and gardening supplies. You also need ideas about what to do. There is help in this book. You can also get ideas about what to do from people who know.

**Preparing** is getting ready. You must prepare spaces where you will plant. You have to get the supplies.

**Taking action** is doing what you need to **plant** and grow fruits and vegetables.

# Think ahead and make a plan

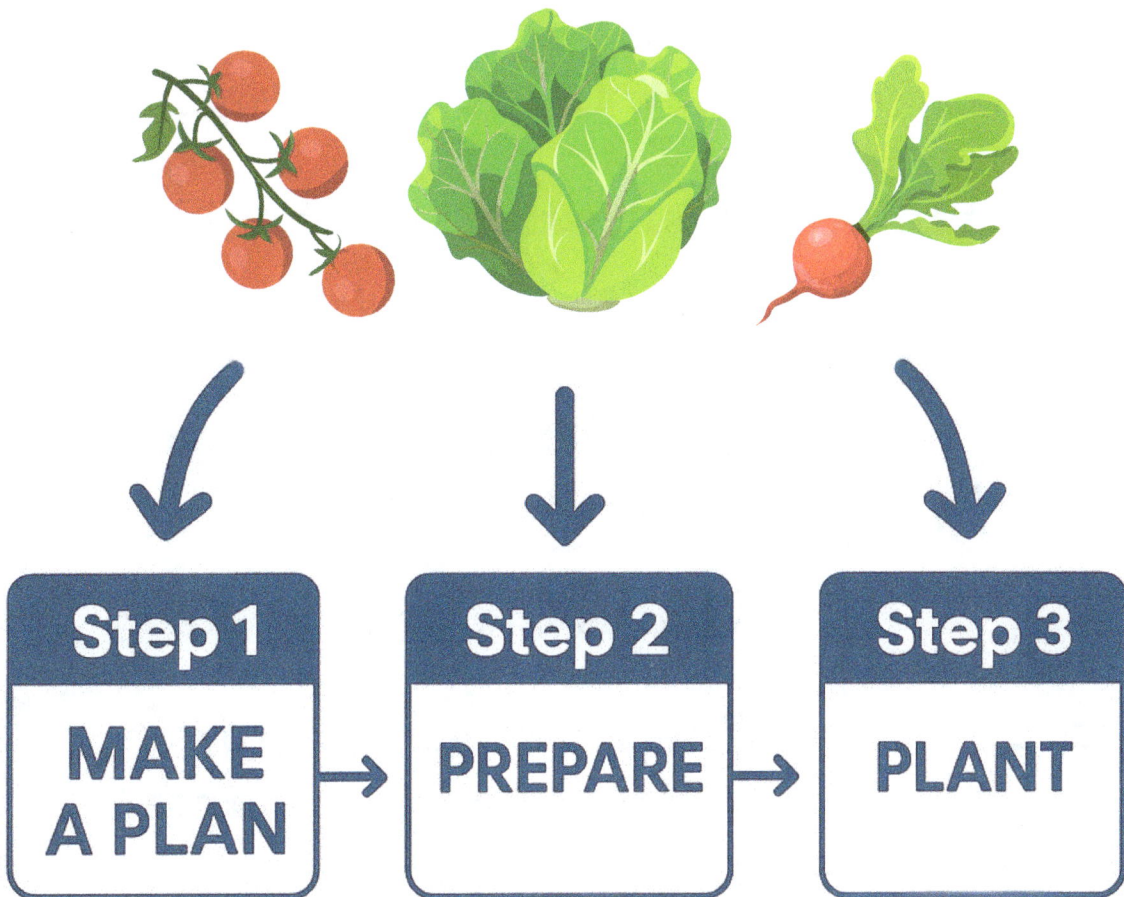

| Step 1 | Step 2 | Step 3 |
|--------|--------|--------|
| MAKE A PLAN | PREPARE | PLANT |

# Planning

Planning includes:

- Figuring out **what** you need to grow tomatoes, lettuce, and radish,

- Thinking about **how** to get the things you need,

- And, thinking about **when** you should do the things you need.

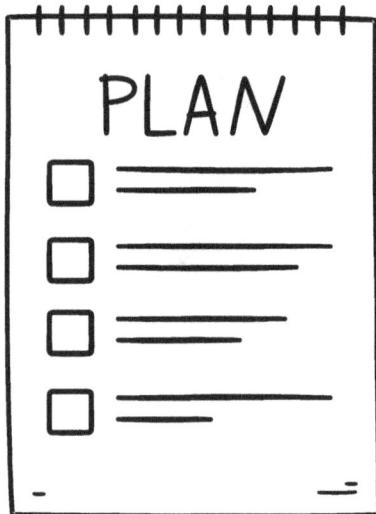

With planning you have to think about things.

What is the weather like?

When is it best to grow different types of plants?

How long does it take for plants to grow?

**Be sure** to check the tags and descriptions of plants. These tell about the type of plant you have, how long it takes to grow, and the kind of weather the plant needs to grow well.

# Planning:  Things you will need

## Plants

- One or two cherry tomato plants
- One or two leaf lettuce plants
- One package of radish seeds

There are many types of cherry tomatoes. They come in different colors.  Some are sweet. Some tomato plants come in a pot with the cage already attached.  Leaf lettuce plants are fun and easy to grow. Leaf lettuce comes in different colors.

**Ask** people who know about the right types of plants and seeds for the area where you live.  These might be people at the garden store, gardeners who live near you, and parents.

# Planning: Things you will need

• Pots with drainage holes

Drainage holes are usually at the bottom of the pot. Drainage holes let extra water out of the pot, so the roots of plants do not get too wet.

• Or you can use a raised bed. A raised bed is a special garden box that is built above the ground. It looks like a sandbox. But instead of sand, a raised bed is filled with soil for growing plants. Water drains through the soil to the ground underneath.

14

# Planning:  Things you will need

- You can also use grow bags.  These can be purchased from a garden store.  With grow bags, the roots of plants get more air.  This is because grow bags are made of fabric where air can flow inside.  Plants grow bigger and stronger with grow bags.

### Make a Grow Bag

Use a plastic laundry basket with holes on the sides.  Ask an adult to help you carefully cut a drainage hole in the bottom of the basket. Always ask an adult when using scissors or cutting tools. Line the inside of the basket with grow bag fabric. Press the fabric down to cover the inside of the basket.  Let a little bit of the fabric fold over the top of the basket.

# Planning:  Things you will need

- You can plant vegetables in the ground too. But the soil must be healthy enough.

- How will you know if the soil is good enough for plants to grow?  You will learn about checking the soil in this book. You will also learn about ways to improve the soil.

- You can also ask parents, neighbors, and gardeners in your area questions to learn more about the soil. You can ask what you can do to make the soil better.

- Ask people at the garden store about the best soil to use for plants.

# Planning: Things you will need

## Gardening Supplies

- A shovel that is the right size to dig a hole in your gardening container or soil.

- Gardening gloves to keep your hands clean and safe.

- Soil that is healthy enough to grow plants. You may already have this in your garden.

- A watering can or hose that is gentle enough to water plants. You must be careful when watering plants. They cannot take in water too fast. Give them a gentle shower when watering.

# Knowing and Growing Tomatoes

## BEFORE YOU PLANT

**GET READY**

# Knowing and Growing Tomatoes

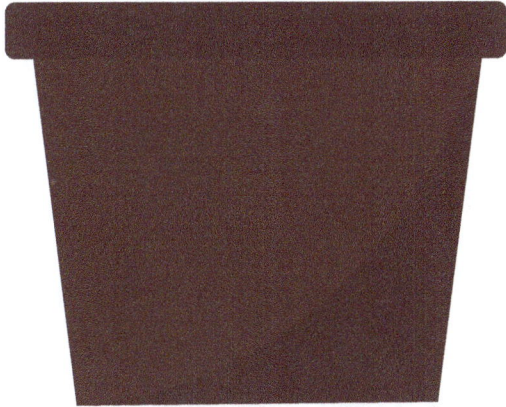

When growing tomatoes in a pot, you will need one that holds at least five gallons. One tomato plant should be in one five-gallon pot.

To check you can put things like soda cans, water bottles, milk cartons, and other things in the empty pot. Then check to see if they add up to five gallons.

1 Gallon = 128 Fluid Ounces

5 Gallons = 640 Fluid Ounces

A standard water bottle size in the United States is 16.9 fluid ounces. This means the pot should be big enough to fit about 38 cans that are 16.9 fluid ounces.

640 divided by 16.9
= 37.86
(rounded up to 38)

19

# Knowing and Growing Tomatoes

## Weather Conditions

Tomatoes grow best when days are warm, and nights are mild.

Plant tomatoes when the temperatures in the **daytime** are between 70 and 85 degrees Fahrenheit (F).

The nighttime temperatures should be between 55 and 70 degrees.

## BEFORE YOU PLANT

Check the weather forecast to see if the temperatures will be good for tomatoes. Use temperatures that are listed in Fahrenheit, (F). Daytime temperatures should be less than 85 degrees.  At nighttime, temperatures should be at least 55 degrees.  These temperatures should happen for ten days straight.

Turn the page to start **"Is it time yet?"**

# Is It Time Yet?

**Keep track of the weather in rows and columns.**

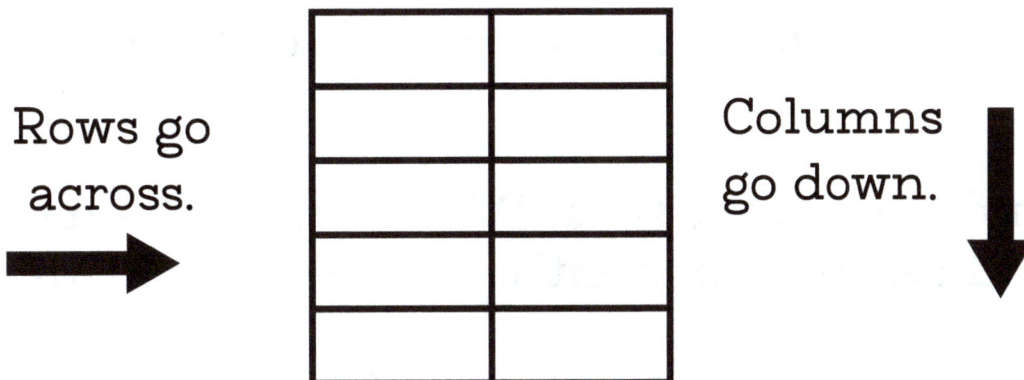

Rows go across. →

Columns go down. ↓

See the next two pages to learn how to use an "Is it time yet?" chart like the one below.

**Is it time yet?**

| Date | Highest Daytime TEMP. | Lowest Nightime TEMP. | Y or N |
|------|------------------------|------------------------|--------|
| May 17 | 70 | 58 | Y |
| May 18 | 76 | 59 | Y |
| May 19 | 76 | 59 | Y |
| May 20 | 75 | 58 | Y |
| May 21 | 76 | 59 | Y |
| May 22 | 74 | 59 | Y |
| May 23 | 69 | 58 | Y |
| May 24 | 70 | 59 | Y |
| May 25 | 72 | 59 | Y |
| May 26 | 70 | 58 | Y |
| | | | |
| | | | |

# Knowing and Growing Tomatoes

## Weather Conditions

**Each day chart the temperature in one row.**

- Under where it says "DATE," write the month and day of the month. An example is May 3.

- Next to the date, write the highest daytime temperature for that day. Next, write the lowest nighttime temperature for the day.

- The weather forecast will tell you the high of the day and the low of the night. Make sure the temperatures are in Fahrenheit (F).

- When the daytime temperature is less than 85 degrees, and the nighttime temperature is more than 55 degrees, put Y for yes in the last column.

- When you do not put Y, write N for no in the last column.

 # Is It Time Yet?

Write down the temperatures until you know it is time to plant.

When you have ten Ys down the last column, with no Ns in between, you are ready to plant.

Y
Y
Y
Y
Y
Y
Y
Y
Y
Y

READY

An "Is it time yet?" chart is on the next page.

Based on what you have learned, decide **when** to start the "Is it time yet" chart.

# Is It Time Yet?

| DATE | Highest DAYTIME TEMP. | Lowest NIGHT TEMP. | Y or N |
|------|----------------------|--------------------|--------|
|      |                      |                    |        |
|      |                      |                    |        |
|      |                      |                    |        |
|      |                      |                    |        |
|      |                      |                    |        |
|      |                      |                    |        |
|      |                      |                    |        |
|      |                      |                    |        |
|      |                      |                    |        |
|      |                      |                    |        |
|      |                      |                    |        |
|      |                      |                    |        |
|      |                      |                    |        |
|      |                      |                    |        |

Extra copies of this table are on pages 99 - 100.

# Black History Notes

Meteorology is the study of weather. Meteorologists help us to know the weather in advance. Knowing the weather in advance helps us to plan when to plant, and how much to water.

**June Bacon-Bercey**

Photo: US National Oceanic and Atmospheric Administration (NOAA)

June Bacon-Bercey, born in 1928, was the first African American woman to earn a degree in meteorology. She worked for the National Weather Service and the Atomic Energy Commission. She was also a television meteorologist during her career.

# Knowing and Growing Tomatoes

## The Soil

Plants like tomatoes live in soil. Plants do better when the soil is good. You want to plant in the best soil you can. If you buy new soil from the garden store, you are starting off with good soil.

You can also test the soil to see if it is good. Soil tests help you find the best places to plant. **Wear gloves to test the soil.** Ask your parents or other adults in charge where you can test the soil. There are different ways to test the soil.

Let us look at **good** versus **bad** soil on the next page.

# Knowing and Growing Tomatoes

## GOOD SOIL

It is soft, fluffy, and a little crumbly.

The color is dark brown.

It smells like after it rains.

It is well drained. Water easily flows down the soil to the roots of the plant.

The soil in the ground has worms.

## BAD SOIL

It is hard and sticky feeling.

It feels and looks like dust or sand.

Sand is **not** for growing plants.

It smells bad, like rotten eggs.

It feels like play dough or clay when wet.

The water does not flow down easily.

There are no worms in the soil in the ground.

# Knowing & Growing Tomatoes

1. The soil should feel soft and fluffy, and a little crumbly.

While wearing gloves, scoop up the soil. Move it around in your glove or on a small shovel. It should seem soft and fluffy. Squeeze it a little. If it crumbles a bit that is a good sign.

2. Look closely at the color.

The soil should have a dark brown color.

# Knowing and Growing Tomatoes

## Testing the Soil

3.  Smell the ground soil.

But **be careful!** Never put your nose in the soil.

Keep your nose about four to six inches away from soil and **sniff gently**.  Do **not** breathe in fast or deep.

The soil should have a smell like the outside after it rains.  Good soil does not smell bad.

4. Have the soil tested.

With the help of an adult, you can search the Internet. Search for something like "soil tests for gardeners near me."  You may find local places to test your soil.  Some might charge a fee to test the soil.

# Knowing and Growing Tomatoes

## Testing the Soil

5.  See if the water drains well in the soil.

Plants need soil that is well drained.  This means that water easily flows down to the roots.

**Test to see if the soil is well drained.**

a.  Take a watering can or hose, and water slowly until water starts to pool. When water starts to pool, stop watering.

b.  Wait one hour.  Then check if the top of the soil is still a little wet.  Wet soil is a little darker than usual.  If you put a stick in wet soil, it looks a little sticky and a little crumbly.

c. The soil on top should be a little wet, but **not** soggy or muddy.  If the soil on top is like mud or soggy, not much water flows down to get to the roots of plants.

# Knowing and Growing Tomatoes

## Testing the Soil

6. Check to see if the soil in the ground has worms.

Worms help the soil stay healthy.   They make tunnels that improve drainage.

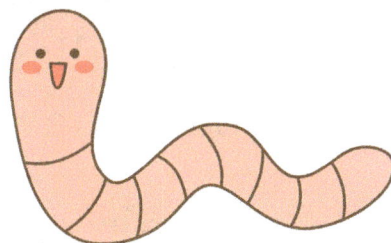

Worms poop after eating dead plants and other things in the soil. These are called **worm castings**. The worm castings have ingredients that help plants grow strong.

Worms may find their way into the soil of outdoor potted plants too.  They often enter through the drainage holes of containers.  They look for soil with food like leaves and dead plant matter.

# Knowing and Growing Tomatoes

## Improving Soil

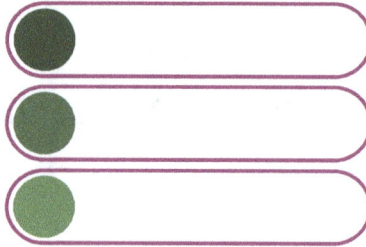

Visit a garden store and ask for help finding the right soil for your plants. Let them know if you are planting in the ground, a raised bed, or in a container. You can buy soil to grow your plants, or you can buy special things called "amendments" to make the soil you already have even better.

You can use a shovel to break up hard soil, and to remove rocks.

You can also make compost. Composting means helping nature break down foods and plants to make soil full of nutrients. But this takes a while. You have to do a lot to make compost.

When you are **not** gardening in a spot, there are things you can do. You can help the soil by covering it with leaves that fall from trees. Let the leaves stay there, and over time, they will break down and turn into soil too. This takes a while, but it is nature's way of giving back to the earth!

# Knowing and Growing Tomatoes

## Find a Spot to Plant

**Find the right spot to plant.**

Tomato plants need between six and eight hours of sunlight a day. To find the right spot, check outside for sunny spots during the day.

Think about where you want to plant. Go outside in the morning and put rocks or other markers down. Place them where the sun hits the ground. There is **no shade** in sunny spots.

Go outside again around lunch time to see if the spot is still sunny. Do this once more a few hours later. Check to see which spots are still sunny.

Try this a couple of times on sunny and clear days. Choose one or more spots that are sunny for six to eight hours.

33

# Knowing and Growing Tomatoes

## Finding a Tomato Plant

You can find a cherry tomato plant at a garden store. Choose the cherry tomato plant you want to grow. Tomatoes come in different colors. Look at the picture on the plant tag or description to see what the plant will look like when it is fully grown. Red, yellow, and orange cherry tomatoes are easier to grow.

Look at the tag or description to see how long it takes for the tomatoes to ripen. A tomato is ripe when it is ready to eat. Check the tag to see how tall the tomato plant will be. The tag also tells how far apart to space the tomato plants. This is needed when planting more than one in the ground.

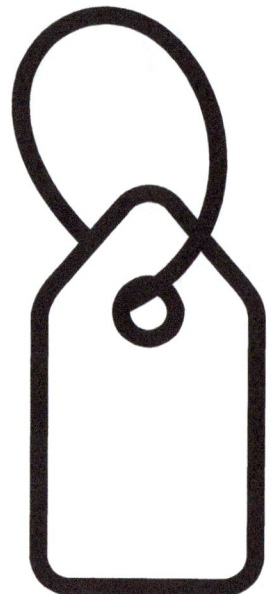

# Knowing and Growing Tomatoes

## Finding a Tomato Plant

Cherry tomato plants from the garden store take about two months to become ripe.

### Stages of Tomato Growth

When you buy a tomato plant from a garden store, it may be in the **vegetative growth** stage. This means it will have leaves but not yellow flowers.

It could also be in the next flowering stage. This is where the plant has yellow flowers. The tomatoes grow from inside of the yellow flowers.

Some tomato plants at the garden store come in a pot with a cage. And all you have to do is water them.

# Knowing and Growing Tomatoes

## Planting

When you are planting tomatoes or other plants in the soil, you should **wear gloves.**

**The hole should be wide enough**.

If you are planting in a pot, you might be able to use your gloved hands to make a hole that is big enough.

Look at each side of the plant, and on the front and back.  Dig a hole that is a little wider than the pot your tomato plant comes with.  Make the hole about one to two inches wider on each side.

You can use a ruler, but it does not have to be exact.

# Knowing and Growing Tomatoes

## Planting

**How deep should the hole be?**

**Measure the height of the tomato plant before you dig the hole.**

The hole should be as deep as **two thirds (2/3)** of the tomato plant.

See more on the next page.

Also, when planting more than one cherry tomato plant in the ground, a general rule is to space them about eighteen inches apart.

George Washington Carver taught us that rotating crops is important to keep the soil healthy. So, the **next time** you plant tomatoes, change the spot.

# Knowing and Growing Tomatoes

## Planting

When planting, it is a good idea to bury **two thirds (2/3)** of the tomato plant into the hole.

Use a ruler to measure the plant from the bottom of the stem to the top of the plant.

Dig around the pot to find the base or bottom of the stem.

Then, imagine the plant divided into three equal parts. You can use a calculator to divide the height by 3.  Then bury **two of the three parts** into the hole.

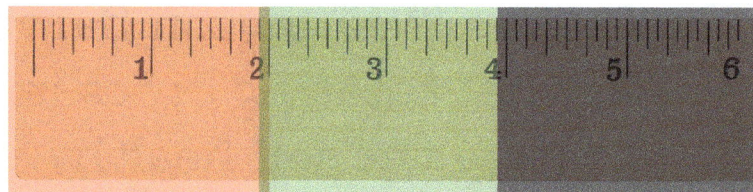

You can also take your best guess about what makes two thirds of the plant.  It does not have to be exact.

# Knowing and Growing Tomatoes

## Planting

There is a reason it is a good idea to bury two thirds of the tomato plant into the hole. It is because tomato plants can grow roots from the stems. Tomato plants are special in this way.

Roots help plants grow big and strong. Roots help the plant eat and drink. Roots take in water and healthy things from the soil. Roots also help the plant stand up on its own.

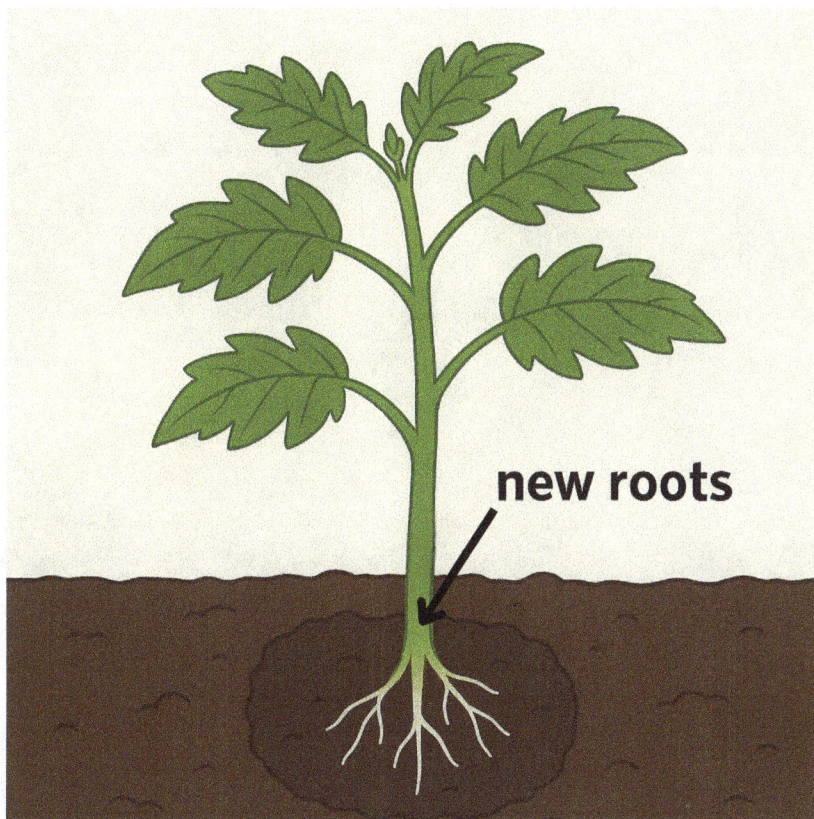

new roots

# Knowing and Growing Tomatoes

## Planting into a Hole

Gently remove the tomato plant from the container it came with. Squeeze the container at the bottom and sides to help loosen the soil. Tip the container to the side.

Do not pull the plant from the top of the leaves. Gently pull the base of the stem, just where the plant comes out of the soil. Remove the plant from the container. Hold on to the bottom and place it into the hole. Cover the part of the plant in the hole with soil.

# Knowing and Growing Tomatoes

Tomato plants need help standing. Tomato plants grow up and out. The plant carries the weight of the growing tomatoes.

Tomato cages help the tomato plant stand. They are round and made of wire. Tomato cages have pointy **stakes** at the bottom that go into the soil.

It is a good idea to put the tomato cage on soon or right after you plant.

Get an adult to help you when putting a cage over a tomato plant. Hold up the cage above the tomato plant. The tomato plant should be in the center of the cage. Gently push the stakes straight down into the soil. Be careful. The stakes go in the soil around the plant.

The stakes and cage should be firmly in place, and not wobbly.

# Knowing and Growing Tomatoes

## Planting

The tomato cage should be the right size. It should fit the plant.

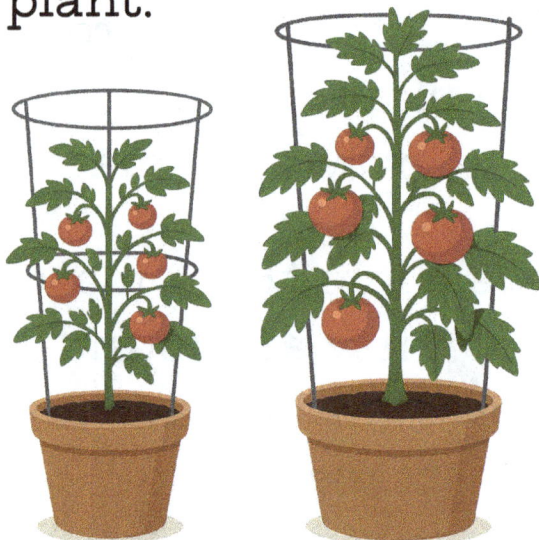

The tag tells you about how tall the tomato plant will be.

Some tomato plants grow about three to four feet tall. In this case the tomato cage should be about three feet tall. The tomato cage should also be about one foot (or twelve inches) wide.

Other tomato plants grow more than six feet tall. These need a bigger cage. They need one that is about five feet tall. The tomato cage should also be one and a half feet (or eighteen inches) wide.

Tomato plants do not need everything to be perfect to grow. But when you take good care of them, they turn out better.

# Knowing and Growing Tomatoes
## Watering

The soil and container where you have planted are the new home for the tomato plant.

Tomato plants need time to get used to this new place. The tomato plant will need more water right after you plant.

It is important to check on tomato plants often to see if they have enough water. The plan for watering tomato plants changes as time goes by.

Sometimes rain will water the plants. But there needs to be enough rain. When it is warmer, tomato plants need more watering than when it is cooler.

It is best to water tomato plants in the morning. Watering in the morning helps plants stay healthy.

# Knowing and Growing Tomatoes
## Watering

Here are some general rules for watering.

Water at the bottom of the plant, where it goes into the soil. Do not water the leaves or stems.

**On day one**, as soon as you plant, water the tomato plant.

Give the tomato plant a good watering. Water a little at a time. Water about a cup or eight fluid ounces at a time. Check to see if the soil is wet to about **six inches** deep.

The soil should be wet about six inches deep.

Use a stick or ruler to check about **six inches** down. When you pull out the stick or ruler, it should have soil that is a little sticky because it is wet.

Do the **same thing on days two and three** after planting as well. Make sure the soil is wet to about **six inches** deep.

# Knowing and Growing Tomatoes
## Watering

Continue to check the soil every day during the **first week**. On **day four** after planting, use a stick to check the soil.

Put a ruler or stick about **two inches** into the soil. **If** the soil is dry or crumbly-looking at the end of the stick, the plant needs watering. **Water to six inches deep**.

**If** the soil still feels wet, the next day check it **two inches** down. Wait until the soil is dry or crumbly looking at two inches down to water again. Water the plant slowly, and to about six inches deep.

Watering tomato plants in the morning helps them stay cool and moist during the day.

# Knowing and Growing Tomatoes
## Watering

### WEEK 2

During the second week, you can water tomato plants about every two to three days. If the weather is on the hotter side, you will need to water more often.

Check the soil. Water tomato plants when the soil is dry about two inches deep. Water to about six inches deep.

Once you start watering, you will see your tomato plant grow.

Tomato plants grow in stages just like people. They go from tiny seeds to full-grown plants.

# Knowing and Growing Tomatoes

## The Harvest

To harvest means to pick the fruits and vegetables you have been growing. You do this when the fruits and vegetables are ripe. Ripe fruits and vegetables are ready to eat.

When tomatoes are ripe, they become the color they are supposed to be. The color should look strong and full and **not** pale or light. There are other things too that tell if tomatoes are ripe.

It tells on the tag when you buy the tomato plant how long it takes for the tomatoes to become ripe. The amount of time listed on the tag for ripening should have passed.

# Knowing and Growing Tomatoes

## The Harvest

- Wait until the tomatoes are the color they are supposed to be.

- A ripe tomato is rich and bright, like someone turned up the color.

- See if it is time to pick the tomato.

To see if a tomato is ready to be picked, hold the tomato in one hand.

In your other hand, hold the part of the stem just above where the tomato is attached to the plant.

Gently twist the tomato to see if it comes off easily.

If it comes off easily, it is ripe and ready to eat.

# Knowing and Growing Tomatoes

## The Harvest

# ENJOY

# Sankofa Notes

Sankofa means to bring important lessons from the past into the present and future. Write down what you liked about knowing and growing tomatoes. What went well for you?

⊢————————————————————————

⊢————————————————————————

⊢————————————————————————

⊢————————————————————————

⊢————————————————————————

# Sankofa Notes

## Carrying Forward Lessons

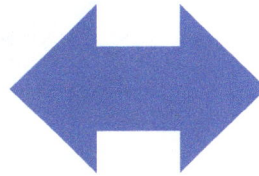

Sankofa means to bring important lessons from the past into the present and future.  What lessons from gardening will you take with you?

| |
| |
| |
| |
| |

# Enjoying The Fruits of Your Labor: A Black History Moment

From The New York Public Library

**Fannie Lou Hamer** was a civil rights activist who encouraged African Americans to grow their own food. She lived during a time when it was a lot harder for Black families to get enough food.

Fannie Lou Hamer created the Freedom Farm Cooperative. She raised money to purchase land so that African Americans could work together to farm and grow their own food.

By learning to grow your own food, you are helping to make her wish come true. She wanted a world where Black children and families could be free, provide food for themselves, and enjoy the rewards of their hard work.

# Knowing and Growing Lettuce

## BEFORE YOU PLANT

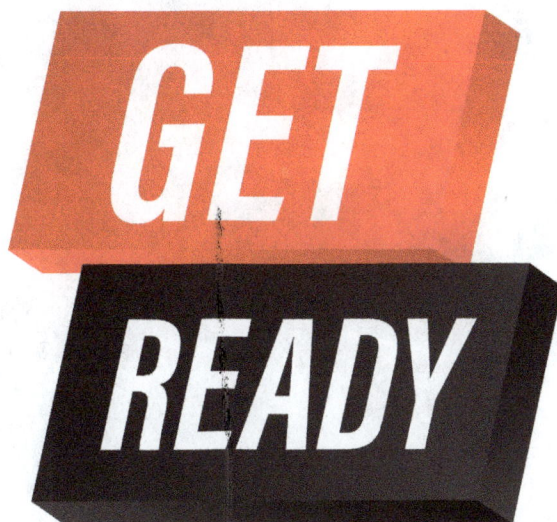

**GET READY**

# Knowing and Growing Lettuce

## Having Room to Grow

One lettuce plant should be in a pot that is at least six to eight inches wide, and six to eight inches deep.

If more than one lettuce plant is in a pot, you will need a bigger one. There should be about six inches of space between lettuce plants.

# Knowing and Growing Lettuce

## Weather Conditions

Lettuce likes cooler weather, but it can still grow when it is a little warmer.

Plant lettuce when **daytime** temperatures are between 60 and 75 degrees Fahrenheit (F).

Plant lettuce when **nighttime** temperatures are higher than 45 degrees.

Check the weather forecast to see if temperatures are good for growing lettuce. Daytime temperatures should be between 60 and 75 degrees, and nighttime temperatures should be more than 45 degrees for about seven days straight.

The daily weather forecast shows the highest temperature during the day and the lowest temperature at night. Use a forecast that lists the temperatures in Fahrenheit (F).

**Is it time yet** to grow lettuce? See the next page.

55

# Is It Time Yet?

**Keep track of the weather in rows and columns.**

Rows go across.

Columns go down.

See the next page to learn how to use an "Is it time yet?" chart like the one below.

### Is it time yet?

| Date | Highest Daytime TEMP. | Lowest Nightime TEMP. | Y or N |
|---|---|---|---|
| May 4 | 65 | 50 | Y |
| May 5 | 64 | 52 | Y |
| May 6 | 71 | 54 | Y |
| May 7 | 62 | 52 | Y |
| May 8 | 64 | 53 | Y |
| May 9 | 72 | 55 | Y |
| May 10 | 71 | 52 | Y |
| | | | |
| | | | |

# Knowing and Growing Lettuce

## Weather Conditions

**Each day chart the temperature in one row.**

Under where it says "DATE," write the month and day of the month. An example is May 3.

Next to the date, write the highest daytime temperature. Next to the daytime temperature write the lowest nighttime temperature.

When the daytime temperature is less than 75 degrees, and the nighttime temperature is higher than 45 degrees, put Y for yes in the last column.

Y
Y
Y
Y
Y
Y
Y

When you do not put Y, write N for no in the last column.

When you have seven Ys down the last column, with no Ns in between, you are ready to plant. Fill in the table on next page.

# Is It Time Yet?

| DATE | Highest DAYTIME TEMP. | Lowest NIGHT TEMP. | Y or N |
|---|---|---|---|
|  |  |  |  |
|  |  |  |  |
|  |  |  |  |
|  |  |  |  |
|  |  |  |  |
|  |  |  |  |
|  |  |  |  |
|  |  |  |  |
|  |  |  |  |
|  |  |  |  |
|  |  |  |  |
|  |  |  |  |
|  |  |  |  |
|  |  |  |  |

Extra copies of this table are on pages 99 - 100.

# Knowing and Growing Lettuce

## The Soil

Lettuce needs good soil too.

**Review pages 26 to 32 that are about the soil.**

Test the soil using the steps given.  You can help improve the soil if needed.

# Knowing and Growing Lettuce

## Find a Spot to Plant

**Lettuce is picky** about the type of sun it needs to grow best.  Review page 55 again to see the type of weather lettuce likes.

Think about if the daily temperatures are on the **cooler side** of what lettuce likes.  An **example** is 45 degrees at night and 65 degrees during the day.

When daily temperatures are on the cooler side, lettuce likes between six and eight hours of sunlight. This means **full sun** in places with no shade.

## Lettuce is picky about the sun it needs.

**Cooler Weather
Full Sun**

**Warmer Weather
Partial Sun**

# Knowing and Growing Lettuce

## Find a Spot to Plant

Think about the time of year you are planting lettuce. Is it on the cooler or warmer side of what lettuce likes?

When daily temperatures are on the **cooler side** for growing lettuce, plant in **full sun** with no shade.

Think about where you want to plant. Go outside in the morning and put rocks or other markers down where the sun is hitting the ground. There **is no shade** in sunny spots.

Go outside again around lunch time to see if the spot is still sunny. Do this once more a few hours later to check to see which spots are still sunny.

Try this a couple of times on sunny and clear days. Choose a spot with six to eight hours of full sun.

# Knowing and Growing Lettuce

## Find a Spot to Plant

Other times, daily temperatures are on the **warmer side** of what lettuce likes.  An example would be a temperature of 75 degrees during the day and 60 degrees during the night.

In these cases, lettuce likes **partial sun**.  With partial sun, lettuce needs **more shade** during the day.  With six hours of sun, lettuce would like three hours of full sunlight with no shade, and three hours of partial sunlight **with** shade.

It is a good idea to give the plant full sunlight in the mornings, and partial sunlight with shade in the afternoons.

## Lettuce is picky about the sun it needs.

**Cooler Weather
Full Sun**

**Warmer Weather
Partial Sun**

# Knowing and Growing Lettuce

## Find a Spot to Plant

When temperatures are on the warmer side of what lettuce likes, find sunny **and** shady spots.

Think about where you want to plant. Go outside in the morning and put rocks or other markers down where the sun is hitting the ground. There is no shade in sunny spots.

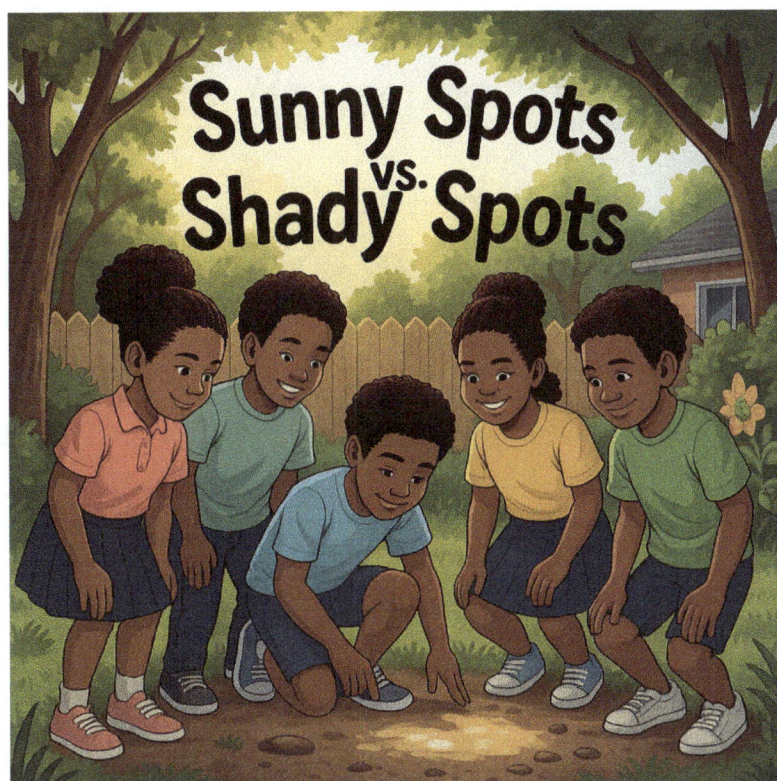

In the afternoon, after 1:00PM, check these same places. Plant lettuce where it is shady in the afternoon. You may have to try several spaces on sunny and clear days to find ones that are sunny in the morning, and shady in the afternoon.

# Knowing and Growing Lettuce

## Finding a Lettuce Plant

A leaf lettuce plant from the garden store takes about one to two months to ripen. Once the lettuce is ripe, it can be picked from the plant and eaten. Look at the tag or description to see how long it takes to ripen.

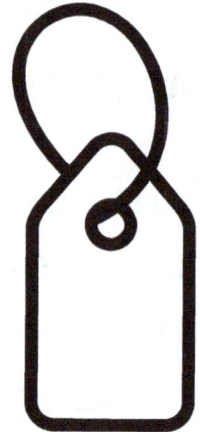

## LETTUCE GROWTH STAGES

When you buy a lettuce plant from a garden store, it will be in the middle stages of growth. These stages are a good time to plant lettuce into another container or the ground.

See the next page for "Dos and Don'ts" when finding a lettuce plant.

# Knowing and Growing Lettuce

## Finding a Lettuce Plant

### DO's

Choose a plant that is bright in color.

The color should be green, or reddish purple when using red leaf lettuce.

Choose plants that are standing upright.

The soil in the pot should be a little moist or damp.

Choose plants with no bugs or holes.

### DON'Ts

Choose a plant that seems dull in color.

Choose plants with brown, yellow or black spots.

Choose plants that are droopy or limp.

Choose plants where the soil is completely dry.

Choose plants that have bugs or holes.

# Knowing and Growing Lettuce

Dig a hole that is a little wider **and** deeper than the **root ball** of the plant.

The **root ball** is the bottom part of the plant.  This is where all the roots are bunched up and hold onto the soil.

Dig a hole about two inches wider **and** two inches deeper than the pot the lettuce came with.

# Knowing and Growing Lettuce

## Planting into a Hole

Gently remove the lettuce plant from the container. Squeeze the container at the bottom and sides to help loosen up things.

Do not pull the plant from the top of the leaves. Tip the container to the side. Gently pull the base of the stem, just where the plant comes out of the soil. Remove the plant from the container. Hold on to the base of the stem and place it into the hole. Cover the part of the plant in the hole with soil.

# Knowing and Growing Lettuce
## Watering

Here are some general rules for watering.

Water the lettuce after planting. **Water gently and slowly.** Lettuce does not like soggy soil. Do not let water pool on top of the soil.

The water should get to the roots. You should water to about **three inches** deep. Use a stick or ruler to check three inches below the soil. It should feel wet.

When you pull out the stick or ruler, it should have soil that is a little sticky three inches deep, because it is wet.

For the first week after planting, check the soil every day. **If** the top inch of soil feels dry, water the lettuce plant. Water gently to about **three inches** deep.

It is a good idea to water plants in the morning, to keep them healthy and cooler during the day.

# Knowing and Growing Lettuce
## Watering

During the **second week** after planting, keep checking every day to see if the lettuce plant needs watering.

When the temperatures are on the warmer side of what lettuce likes, more watering is needed.

Check to see if the top inch of soil is dry.  When the top inch of soil is dry it needs to be watered to about **four inches** deep.

During the **third week**, you can check the lettuce plant every couple of days to see if it needs watering.  When the top of the soil (about an inch down) is dry, water gently to about **four inches** deep.

Sometimes the rain helps us out. When it rains, we do not have to water as much.

# Knowing and Growing Lettuce

## The Harvest

Harvesting means you can pick the lettuce leaves because they are ready to eat. Harvesting happens when the lettuce is ripe. The information on the tag or description that comes with the plant, tells about how long it takes for the lettuce to become ripe.

A general rule is to pick lettuce leaves when they are six inches long.

When picking lettuce, pick the outer and larger leaves first. These are the ripest. When picking leaves, use clean scissors or simply pinch the leaves to take them off. Ask an adult to help.

It is best to pick lettuce leaves **before** you see yellow flowers. The yellow flowers mean the lettuce is past being ripe. And the lettuce will not taste as good. If you see yellow flowers coming in, pick the leaves.

# Knowing and Growing Lettuce

## The Harvest

ENJOY

# Sankofa Notes

Sankofa means to bring important lessons from the past into the present and future. Write down what you liked about knowing and growing lettuce. What things went well for you?

# Sankofa Notes

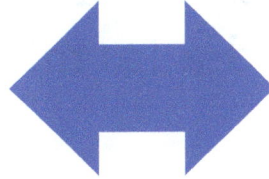

Sankofa means to bring important lessons from the past into the present and future.  What lessons from gardening will you take with you?

# Black History Notes

## Henry Blair (1807 - 1860)

Henry Blair was the second African American to receive a patent from the United States. Henry Blair invented a farming tool that planted corn seeds.

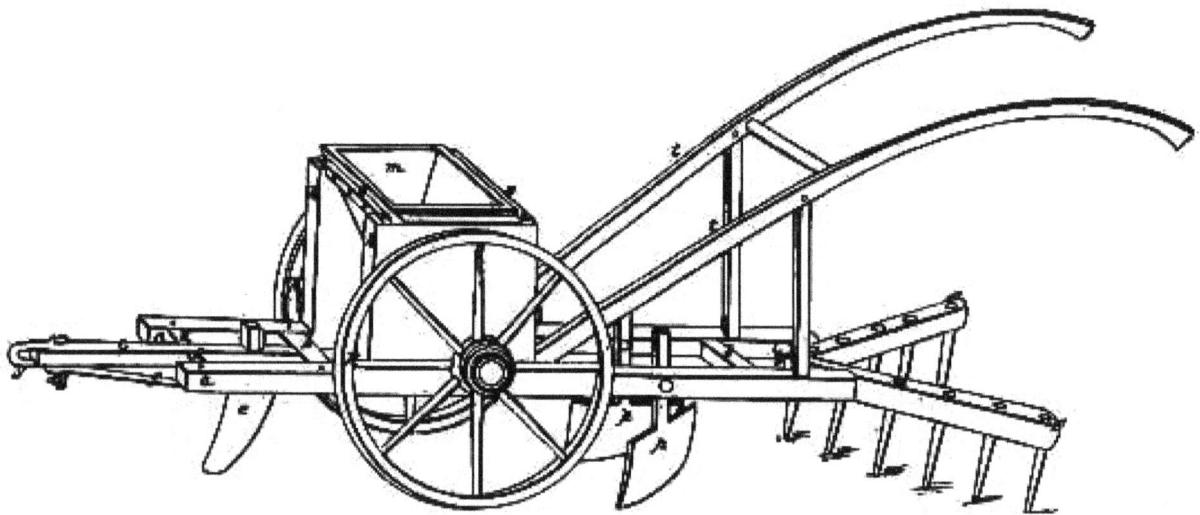

The invention made holes where seeds could be planted. The invention also had a rake to cover the seeds after they were planted. This made it easier to plant seeds.

His other invention helped to break up the soil so that it was loose for planting. This made it easier to plant seeds that would grow.

# Knowing and Growing Radish

## BEFORE YOU PLANT

# Knowing and Growing Radish

## Having Room to Grow

radish

It is best to grow radish from seeds. Radish seeds should be planted in a container that is about six inches deep.

Plant a row of radish seeds if you can.  You will need a pot where you can have **one inch of space** in between each hole.

# Knowing and Growing Radish

## Weather Conditions

Radish grows well during cool days and even cooler nights. Check the weather forecast to see if temperatures are good for planting radish seeds.

Plant radish seeds when **daytime** temperatures are between 60 and 75 degrees Fahrenheit (F).

Plant radish seeds when **nighttime** temperatures are above 45 degrees.

Daytime temperatures should be between 60 and 75 degrees, and nighttime temperatures should be higher than 45 degrees for seven days straight.

The daily weather forecast tells the high for the day and the low during the night. Use a forecast that lists the temperatures in Fahrenheit (F).

Is it time to grow radish? See the next page.

# Is It Time Yet?

**Keep track of the weather in rows and columns.**

Rows go across. →

Columns go down. ↓

See the next page to learn how to use an "Is it time yet?" chart like the one below.

**Is it time yet?**

| Date | Highest Daytime TEMP. | Lowest Nightime TEMP. | Y or N |
|------|------------------------|------------------------|--------|
| 9/26 | 75 | 57 | Y |
| 9/27 | 75 | 57 | Y |
| 9/28 | 74 | 56 | Y |
| 9/29 | 74 | 56 | Y |
| 9/30 | 74 | 56 | Y |
| 10/1 | 73 | 55 | Y |
| 10/2 | 73 | 55 | Y |
|  |  |  |  |
|  |  |  |  |

# Knowing and Growing Radish

## Weather Conditions

**Each day chart the temperature in one row.**

Under where it says "DATE," write the month and day of the month. An example is May 3.

Next to the date, write the highest daytime temperature. Next to the daytime temperature write the lowest nighttime temperature.

When the daytime temperature is between 60 and 75 degrees, and the nighttime temperature is higher than 45 degrees, put Y for yes in the last column.

When you do not put Y, write N for no in the last column.

Y
Y
Y
Y
Y
Y
Y

READY

When you have seven Ys down the last column, with no Ns in between you are ready to plant. Fill in the table on next page.

# Is It Time Yet?

| DATE | Highest DAYTIME TEMP. | Lowest NIGHT TEMP. | Y or N |
|------|------|------|------|
|  |  |  |  |
|  |  |  |  |
|  |  |  |  |
|  |  |  |  |
|  |  |  |  |
|  |  |  |  |
|  |  |  |  |
|  |  |  |  |
|  |  |  |  |
|  |  |  |  |
|  |  |  |  |
|  |  |  |  |
|  |  |  |  |
|  |  |  |  |
|  |  |  |  |

Extra copies of this table are on pages 99 - 100.

# Knowing and Growing Radish

## The Soil

Radish seeds need good soil too.

**Review pages 26 to 32 to learn more about the soil.**

Test the soil using the steps provided. You can help improve the soil if needed.

# Knowing and Growing Radish

## Find a Spot to Plant

The radish plant needs six hours of sunlight a day. To find the right spot, check outside on sunny and clear days for sunny spots during the day.

Think about where you want to plant. Go outside in the morning and put rocks or other markers down. Place them where the sun hits the ground. There is **no shade** in sunny spots.

Go outside again around lunch time to see if the spot is still sunny. Do this once more a few hours later. Check which spots are still sunny.

You may have to check for the right spot a couple of times.

Choose one or more spots that are sunny for six hours a day.

# Knowing and Growing Radish

## Finding Radish Seeds

Radish seeds grow fast, with most producing radish in about one month. Some types of radish seeds grow faster than others. Check the tag or description to see how long it takes for radishes to grow.

It is a good idea to check the date of the radish seeds. Look for radish seeds that have been packaged during the current year. Or get radish seeds packaged the year before.

# fresh

# DATE

You want radish seeds that are fresh.

# Knowing and Growing Radish

## Planting

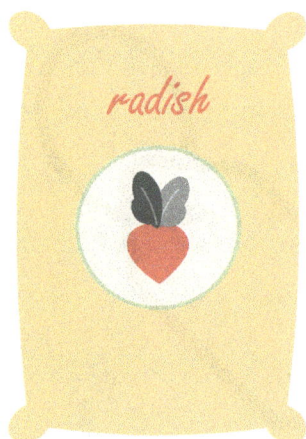

The hole to plant the radish seeds should be about one half (1/2) of an inch **deep**. The hole should be wide enough for the seed to fit.

With a pack of seeds, you will be able to plant one or more **rows** of radish.

The space in between the holes to plant radish seeds should be one inch.

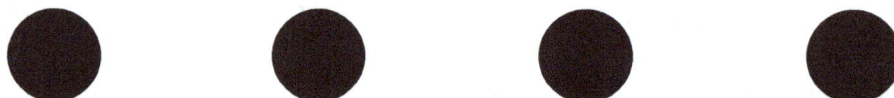

● ● ● ●

With two or more rows, the rows should be about three inches apart.

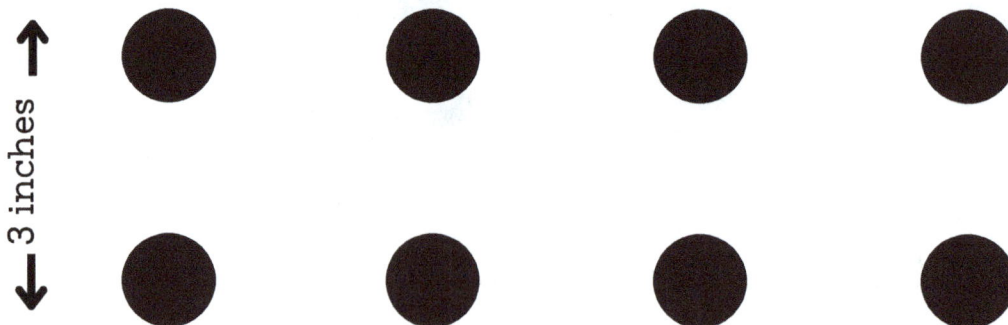

↑
3 inches
↓

● ● ● ●

● ● ● ●

# Knowing and Growing Radish

## Planting into a Hole

Put **one** seed in each hole.  Cover the seeds with soil.  Not all the seeds will grow but many of them should.

# Knowing and Growing Radish
## Watering

Here are some general rules for watering.

Be **extra** careful when watering radish seeds. You want the seeds to stay in place. The water should not splash too hard.

Use a watering can or a cup. Pour very slowly. Do not let water pile on top of the soil.

Water until **two inches** below the soil is **moist**. This means the soil should feel just a little wet. Check with a stick or ruler. Then feel it to see if the soil is just a little wet **two inches** deep.

Check the soil each day. If the top of the soil feels dry, water the plant so that it is moist **two inches** down.

As the radish grows, it begins to change. As it changes you can change how you water.

# Knowing and Growing Radish

## Watering

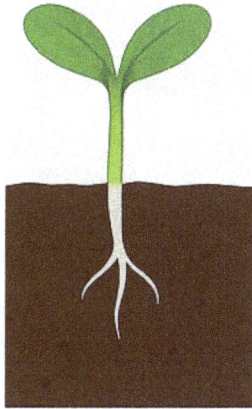

**Sprout**

In about a week after planting seeds, you will see **sprouts**. These are not yet leaves. They are tiny, and light in color. Sprouts are like baby leaves. The edges of sprouts are smooth.

Continue to check the top of the soil every day.

When the **top of the soil** is dry, water the sprouts about **two inches** deep. Be gentle. The soil should feel **moist**, or just a little wet.

# Knowing and Growing Radish

## Watering

Soon you will see real leaves on the plant.  Real leaves have a different look and shape.

They have a "midrib" or thick vein running through the center. Smaller veins come out from the midrib.

**Leaf**

As the plant develops roots, the leaves continue to mature.  The midrib gets thicker. The edges become more jagged or zigzag.

As the plant grows, and has more leaves, check the soil often. Wait until the **top of the soil** is dry.  Then water gently, about **two to three inches** deep.  The soil should be **moist** two to three inches deep.

**Root Growing**

# Knowing and Growing Radish

## Watering

Change how much you water depending on the weather. If it rains, water less. When it is hotter and sunny, water more.

When it is windy, you should water more too. Radishes do not have deep roots. Wind can dry out the roots.

As the radish matures, the roots grow larger. Check the soil often. When the top of the soil is dry, water to make the soil feel **moist**, two to three inches deep.

The soil should not feel soggy or too wet.

# Knowing and Growing Radish

## The Harvest

Fruits and vegetables are ripe and ready to eat at harvest time. Fruits and vegetables should be picked when ripe.

Most radishes are ripe in about one month. But some larger radishes take longer. Read the tag or description on the package of radish seeds to find out.

The amount of time listed on the tag for ripening should have passed before the radish is picked.

A ripe radish is also the color it is supposed to be.

The part of the radish you eat grows underneath the soil. As it matures, you will see some of the round part of the vegetable come up from underneath the soil.

See more on the next page.

# Knowing and Growing Radish

## The Harvest

When the radish is ripe, part of the vegetable will peek out from underneath the soil. And the vegetable will be about one inch across the top.

A ripe radish will be round and firm when you squeeze it. To be sure it is ripe, you must pull it out of the soil.

Hold the radish gently by the bottom of the leaves. Wiggle it back and forth just a little to help it loosen. Slowly pull up the radish in a straight line.

Pick radishes as soon as they are ripe. If you wait too long, the radishes will not taste fresh.

# Knowing and Growing Radish

## The Harvest

ENJOY

# Sankofa Notes

Sankofa means to bring important lessons from the past into the present and future.  Write down what you liked about knowing and growing radish.  What things went well for you?

# Sankofa Notes

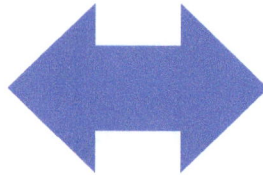

Sankofa means to bring important lessons from the past into the present and future.  What lessons from gardening will you take with you?

# Dr. Marie Clark Taylor

Dr. Marie Clark Taylor was born in 1911. She was the first African American woman to earn a Ph.D. in botany. Botany is the scientific study of plants. Dr. Clark focused on what is called "photomorphogenesis." This word kind of sounds like "foh-toh-mor-FAH-jeh-nuh-sis." It is the study of how light changes the way plants flower.

Dr. Clark helped gardeners and farmers alike to know how they could use light indoors and outdoors to grow plants better. She was also an educator. She taught at Howard University. She encouraged African Americans to get an education in the sciences.

# Ron Finley
# Gardener & Community Activist

Photo by U.S. Embassy New Zealand, licensed under CC BY 2.0.
https://creativecommons.org/licenses/by/2.0/

Ron Finley, a community activist and Master Gardener, is known for changing spaces into community gardens. A community garden is a place where people in the neighborhood come together to grow plants, fruits, and vegetables. Community gardens are a place where people share the work and food.

Ron Finley believes there is power in growing your own food. It connects people to nature and feeds them too. Ron Finley has worked to improve the lives of Black people through community gardens. He is carrying forward the wishes of Fannie Lou Hamer.

# Yield in Life and Gardening

**Yield** is what you get back based on what you do. One example of a high yield is planting ten seeds and having ten huge plants in return.

Yield is like your harvest. It is what you get after working and waiting for something. Yield is not just for gardening. You have a yield in other areas too such as in school, with sports and even friendships.

It takes time to learn what to do, and what not to do to get a good yield. You learn about what to do and not do when you try. **A part of your yield is what you learn**. Trying is how you grow better.

By learning you develop strategies. A strategy is a good plan for what to do. But you should know why it is a good plan. And you must take action.

You do not have to figure everything out on your own. Ask questions of people who know. Learn from others.

# Sankofa Sprouts:
# The Salad Bowl Project

# Is It Time Yet?

| DATE | Highest DAYTIME TEMP. | Lowest NIGHT TEMP. | Y or N |
|------|----------------------|--------------------|--------|
|      |                      |                    |        |
|      |                      |                    |        |
|      |                      |                    |        |
|      |                      |                    |        |
|      |                      |                    |        |
|      |                      |                    |        |
|      |                      |                    |        |
|      |                      |                    |        |
|      |                      |                    |        |
|      |                      |                    |        |
|      |                      |                    |        |
|      |                      |                    |        |
|      |                      |                    |        |
|      |                      |                    |        |

# Is It Time Yet?

| DATE | Highest DAYTIME TEMP. | Lowest NIGHT TEMP. | Y or N |
|------|----------------------|--------------------|--------|
|      |                      |                    |        |
|      |                      |                    |        |
|      |                      |                    |        |
|      |                      |                    |        |
|      |                      |                    |        |
|      |                      |                    |        |
|      |                      |                    |        |
|      |                      |                    |        |
|      |                      |                    |        |
|      |                      |                    |        |
|      |                      |                    |        |
|      |                      |                    |        |
|      |                      |                    |        |
|      |                      |                    |        |

# About The Author

Dr. Leslie K. Grier has been a university educator for over 30 years. Her expertise is in Child and Adolescent Development. A central focus of her work is supporting the growth and well-being of African American children and youth.

Dr. Grier is dedicated to creating enriching and engaging activities that promote positive youth development. This book reflects her personal and professional expertise across several areas, including moral and character development, cognitive and self-development, as well as her training as a Master Gardener.

Dr. Grier has worked with and for out-of-school time programs across decades. She has served as a trainer of staff who support children's growth and learning beyond the classroom. You can learn more about Dr. Grier's work through LinkedIn, https:// www.linkedin.com/in/lesliekgrier/.

www.ingramcontent.com/pod-product-compliance
Lightning Source LLC
Chambersburg PA
CBHW081339090426
42737CB00017B/3212